Cooking
with
Cannabis

WHY THIS BOOK WAS WRITTEN

I have read the few existing marijuana cookbooks and am deeply disappointed with them. In nearly every one of these the author has simply taken a dozen or so ordinary recipes from a standard cookbook, appended the line: "Add ½ cup of grass" to each, and sold it to the public for ten times what it is worth. Worse yet, these books display a total ignorance of the physical and chemical nature of cannabis and how it is absorbed into the system. They have even overlooked such elementary matters as whether the flavor of grass harmonizes or clashes with the other ingredients. If you have been following the instructions in these books, you have most likely been wasting your hard-earned dope.

Notice to Reader

The Art and Science of

Cooking with Cannabis

The Most Effective Methods of Preparing Food & Drink with Marijuana, Hashish & Hash Oil

by Adam Gottlieb

20TH CENTURY ALCHEMIST

RONIN Publishing, Inc.
Berkeley CA

Cooking with Cannabis

978-091417155-3
Copyright 1973, 1993 by 20th Century Alchemist
(Originally published by High Times/Level Press)

Cover Design: Bonnie Smetts
Cover Photographs: Harlan Ang
Cover Construction: Generic Typography

Published by:
Ronin Publishing, Inc.
Post Office Box 22900
Oakland CA 94609

Distributed by:
Publishers Group West

Printed in the United States of America

Table of Contents

INTRODUCTION

Although this book contains numerous recipes, it is not intended to be merely another cookbook or recipe collection. Instead it is designed to serve as a guidebook to teach the reader the nature of cannabis, how it combines with different foods, how it is best assimilated in the human digestive tract, and how he can get the most highs for his money.

The first section of this book compares the results of ingesting cannabis to those from smoking it. The second section explains the physical and chemical nature of cannabis and how it is most effectively digested. The third section describes the concoction of the basic materials, such as canna-butter (Sacred Ghee) and cannabis tar, which are called for in many of the recipes. The fourth section is devoted to some of the most suitable dishes which may be prepared from these materials.

We have covered most of the general types of preparations, though certainly not all of the possible recipes. A reading of this book plus a little practice should impart to the reader sufficient knowledge and understanding with which to devise his own cannabinated culinary creations.

EATING IT VERSUS SMOKING IT

Smoking is one of the many bizarre rituals of mankind. It is practiced universally, more or less, in both primitive and sophisticated societies. Who can say whether it is natural or not? Perhaps, at least for some of our species, it is as much a genetic imperative to smoke as it is for spiders to spin and lemmings to drown. Many of us feel, however, that it is not in the best interest of our lungs to inhale vast volumes of cinders. The heat, tars and harsh smoke from any material, be it tobacco, pot or gentle herb, irritates, interferes with oxygen intake and may hasten pulmonary disorders in persons predisposed to these.

The logical alternative to smoking grass is to ingest it. Convenience, however, often motivates our choice. It is simpler to light a joint than to spend an hour over a hot stove and another hour waiting for the product of our labor to take effect. Furthermore, many of us are so programmed for compulsive smoking that it is unlikely that we would change the pattern for any reason so minor as the well-being of our breathing apparatus. So, unless the reader is some kind of health nut with a fetish about maintaining the function of his lungs, why would any decent, normal, pot-smoking citizen want to switch to eating?

Well, the author is not trying to talk anyone into or out of anything, but it may be enlightening to examine the relative advantages and disadvantages of these two methods of getting stoned.

Smoking, as we have already indicated, is irritating to the throat and lungs. If one is already a user of tobacco, he will at least be mentally inured to taking in smoke. If one is not a cigarette smoker, he will probably fail to inhale the pot smoke properly and in sufficient volumes to achieve the desired state. The ingestion of grass is hedonistic rather than masochistic. Ingested in normal amounts, there are no unpleasant side effects. Consumed in excessive quantities, it may cause a listless feeling and bloodshot eyes the following day.

When cannabis is smoked, the effect is almost instantaneous. Some so-called "creeper" grasses may take five minutes or so to come on completely, but some of the high is usually felt right away. The high from smoking usually lasts from one to two and a half hours, and can be recaptured when it is waning by taking a few more tokes.

When cannabis is ingested, a person must wait thirty minutes to an hour and a half before the first stages of the high are even noticed. After this, the euphoric state continues to increase. It may then last from four to eight hours, and in some cases even longer. This long high can be of great value to a person who is going to be in a place where he cannot conveniently re-stone himself with the difficult-to-conceal smoke. It is always such a contra-hedonistic bother, for instance, to try to sneak a few hasty booster tokes in the toilet stalls during the intermission at a double feature. If the theatergoer ingests rather than smokes his pot, he can stay deliciously high even through an entire Wagnerian opera and still feel like he's in Valhalla upon arriving home.

Although ingested cannabis may take as much as 90 minutes to take effect, most of the recipes in this book are designed to work more swiftly. Several of them may even give the gourmet the first noticeable buzz within fifteen minutes.

Because of their different avenues of absorption, the psychopharmacological effects of ingested cannabis are bound to be somewhat different than those from the smoked material. A good amount of the active components are altered or destroyed during combustion when smoked. The various enzymes and other digestive fluids which must work on the cannabis resins before they can be assimilated alter the structure of the active materials somewhat, and no doubt also the subtle qualities of the high. These differences, though they are subtle and perhaps too susceptible to subjective description to be reported here, will be clearly observable even to the novice connoisseur. Other differences which are more easily described are due to the delayed reaction after ingestion. The effects here will be less pronounced during the initial stages than those from smoking. But as the minutes progress, the "hash eater's" high may become far more overwhelming than anything that the smoker has ever experienced. This may be furthered by the fact that the eater does not get the same immediate signals which tell the smoker that he has had enough. So when he finally comes on, he may really come on—and still keep coming on.

For any and all of the above reasons, ingested cannabis is often more hallucinogenic than the smoke. Spatial distortions, macroscopia (objects appearing larger than normal), and microscopia (appearing smaller) are also more likely to occur. One should keep this in mind if he is planning to drive a vehicle or take on any task which demands accurate perception, judgment and response.

The ritual of rolling a joint or packing a pipe and passing it among a small circle of friends has its undeniable magic. But so does the alchemy of the kitchen and the pleasures of sharing good food with good companions.

One probable advantage of smoking is that it is virtually impossible to overdose in this manner. If a person has smoked too much he will either stop or pass out (hopefully not in bed while holding a lighted joint). One may eat ten times too much and still be eating more before the first effects of the high have even arrived. If he does so, he may eventually lose consciousness for anywhere from 12 to 48 hours, depending upon how much was taken. Unless the consumer is a daring astronaut of inner space who thrives upon bold and sudden leaps into uncharted regions of expanded or deflated consciousness, we generally recommend that the average gourmet exercise some caution when trying to determine the outer limits of his drug tolerance. When beginning to experiment with doses of any unfamiliar material, the best rule, of course, is to start with small amounts and increase gradually as needed.

The Nature
of Cannabis

GETTING THE MOST OUT OF IT

To derive the best and most economical results from cannabinated cuisine, we must keep in mind several facts about the physical and chemical nature of cannabis and how it is broken down and absorbed in the digestive tract. It is not the author's intention to burden or confound the reader with too many of the complexities of science. Yet a rudimentary understanding of some details will be of value in making certain decisions which will give the best results for the least investment.

SOLUBILITY OF CANNABIS

THC, the active substance in grass and hash, is not soluble in water; it is soluble in oils, fats and alcohols. This has been known for thousands of years. Recipes from India and other hash-eating civilizations usually require that the ganja be sautéed in butter or ghee (clarified butter) before combining it with the other ingredients. Still, in the enlightened Twentieth Century, we find otherwise intelligent people boiling, and often only steeping, the leaves, seeds and stems of marijuana in water and drinking cup after cup in pursuit of a high that may never arrive. Then they discard the leaves, which, though soggy, are still potent. If the grass is of excellent quality and has much resin on the outside, it is possible, after strenuous boiling, that a portion of these resins will be softened by the heat and will float out into the tea water. Clearly, though, boiling in water is not an efficient way to extract oil-soluble materials.

Most of the recipes in this writing involve some form of extraction of the cannabis resins into an oil or alcohol medium. This is accomplished by any of the following methods: soaking or boiling in alcohol; sautéing or boiling in oil or butter; combining, uncooked, with oil or butter; combining, heated or unheated, with an oil/water emulsion such as milk. Milk contains butter fats in emulsion with water. Cannabis materials can be boiled in milk and will dissolve into these fats. This emulsion solubility is the basis of the ancient beverage from India known as *bhang*.

DIGESTION OF CANNABIS

There are several ways that a person can ingest cannabis with varying degrees of effectiveness. The simplest, though not the most appetizing, is to chew up and swallow either 5 to 20 grams of marijuana, ½ to 2 grams of hashish, or $1/10$ to ½ gram of hash oil. These amounts are subject to wide variation because of the vastly different potency grades of the products available and the differences in individual tolerances. When these materials are taken straight (on an empty stomach, of course), you may have to wait an hour or more, depending upon the activity of your digestive system, before the initial effects are experienced. It takes less cannabis and less time when the material has been properly dissolved in a suitable medium. The second point, therefore, is akin to the first. **THC is more efficiently assimilated if it has been dissolved in fats or alcohol.**

When fats or oils are ingested, the liver receives a signal to secrete bile, which is then concentrated in the gall bladder and ejected into the duodenum. Bile is a viscid, alkaline fluid which aids in the emulsification, digestion and absorption of fats. Cannabis does stimulate bile flow to some extent. But if cannabis resins are taken into the system without the presence of fats, there may not be enough bile secreted to bring about their complete assimilation. Eventually, in about two to four times as many minutes, some percentage of the resins will be assimilated.

When food is taken into the stomach it is churned about while hydrochloric acid and enzymes begin its digestion. After the contents of the stomach become liquefied, small amounts of it are ejected into the duodenum at 20-second intervals until a certain amount accumulates. Then this process of ejection slows down. Some very small quantity of fat may now be absorbed directly into the blood through the intestinal capillaries. Next the bile begins its work, emulsifying the fat (dispersing it in water in miniscule droplets) and rendering some of the fatty acids water-soluble. Now a greater amount of these fats can be assimilated through the duodenum. Any which are not are digested in the small intestine by pancreatic lipase (an enzyme). As the digesting food is passed from the duodenum to the lower portions of the small intestine, more of the stomach's gastric contents are ejected into the duodenum and similarly acted upon. The total process of emptying the stomach may take from one to four hours.

Note: there is a rumor that vegetarians do not get as stoned on grass as meat eaters. This notion is not absolutely without foundation; it is merely a distortion of the truth. It has been noted several times in scientific literature dating back at least to the early nineteenth century that while carnivorous animals (fish, dogs, swine, vultures, crows, etc.) invariably and speedily exhibit the intoxicating influence of marijuana, the graminivorous ones (vegetarian grazers), such as the horse, deer, monkey, goat, sheep, and cow, experience but trivial effects from any dose administered. Human beings are capable of adapting to either vegetarian or carnivorous diets. The personal eating habits of an individual, no matter how long-standing, have no influence whatsoever upon his ability to enjoy the pleasures of cannabis.

ALCOHOL AND SUGAR

An alcohol solution of the cannabis resins is very readily assimilated even in the absence of digestive secretions. The stomach serves largely as a food reservoir in which food is prepared for further digestion. Only a few substances, such as water, alcohol and certain drugs, are absorbed directly through this organ. Alcohol is rather swiftly absorbed through the stomach lining and will act as a vehicle to carry into the system other substances with which it is combined. Because honey and other sugars are rapidly absorbed into the bloodstream through the intestinal capillaries, they may also serve to some extent as an assimiliation vehicle. But since THC does not dissolve in sugars, the degree of absorption is rather limited.

The signal for the stomach to slow down the process of ejecting its contents into the duodenum is caused by a hormone (enterogastrone). This hormone is released from the intestinal mucosa when sugars and/or fats are present in the small intestine. If too much sugar is present, the fats containing the active resins will be detained longer in the stomach. From this information we may summarize another guidepoint: **The presence of a little sugar in alcohol or in an oil-based confection may somewhat facilitate the assimilation of the THC. Too much sugar, however, can interfere with the digestion of the fats and their payload of THC.**

CHOICE OF CUISINE

A prefatory comment has already been made about the foolishness of most marijuana cookbooks. Some of their recipes are for such esophagus-expanding delights as marijuana in spaghetti or hashish stroganoff. Now imagine a stomach full of spaghetti or stroganoff with several grams of cannabis mixed up in it. After two or three hours, how much of this grand dinner will have been absorbed into the body?

One-fourth? Maybe even a third, if you have the digestive juices of a billy goat. Quite clearly, that is also how much of the homogeneously dispersed cannabis resins will have been assimilated. Most of them will still be in the bulky wad of food inching its sluggish way through thirty feet of intestines. This may have some value in that the gradual assimilation will help to maintain your high for several hours longer, provided that you got enough in you to get stoned on initially. The absorption rate of your cannabinated food throughout its alimentary journey will be more or less as follows: ⅓ assimilated during the first 3 to 4 hours for the initial high, ⅓ gradually absorbed during the next 6 to 8 hours to sort of maintain the high, ⅓ unassimilated materials, which are ultimately sacrificed to the city sewage system. If you want to flush 30 to 40 percent of your overpriced grass and hash down the commode, those recipes will show you how. If you want to get bigger, better, and longer-lasting highs for less investment, then read on.

From what we have just discussed we may establish a third guidepoint: **A little of the right kind of food will aid in the assimilation of the cannabis resins; too much food will merely dilute its potency and waste much of it.**

For the same reason that cannabis is best combined with small morsels rather than huge meals, these morsels should not be taken on a stomach that is already full.

It might be added that the active resins of cannabis are rendered more soluble (even slightly water-soluble) in an alkaline situation. An acid condition interferes with their solubility. Indications are that the resin is best absorbed under the influence of the alkaline juices of the upper part of the small intestine. Absorption in the lower intestine is probably quite minimal. Any further absorption occurring here will not give an additional high, but will merely perpetuate a sluggish hangover and state of listlessness.

EFFECTS OF COOKING ON CANNABIS

The question is sometimes asked: "What is the effect of cooking heat upon cannabis? Will it destroy potency?"

Under normal circumstances, there is no appreciable loss of potency from cooking. For the most part, temperatures which would burn or destroy the active principle would as quickly ruin the recipe itself.

Losses of THC potency are usually the result of oxidation. Unless cannabis is kept in an airless environment, it will be subject to oxidation. In a freezer the rate of oxidation is almost nullified. At room temperature (68°F) oxidation is quite gradual. Ten percent may be lost over a period of several months. At higher temperatures, in the tropics, for instance, this depreciation is only slightly higher. If the cannabis is kept in a very hot place, say 150° or more, a more substantial loss of potency may be expected during the same amount of time.

Cooking temperatures will accelerate the oxidizing process, but the lengths of time usually involved are too brief for much loss to occur. It has been suggested that the amount of marijuana be increased to compensate for longer cooking periods as follows:

Temperature – Degrees F

Minutes	150	200	250	300
30	20	22	24	26
60	22	24	26	28
90	24	26	28	31
120	26	28	31	34

Grams of marijuana

There is no harm nor even likelihood of overindulgence from these slight increases.

In many instances, it is possible that cooking will increase the potency of marijuana. In freshly harvested hemp much, and sometimes all, of its THC is present in the form of tetrahydrocannabinolic acid. The percentage depends upon such factors as time of harvest and the climate in which it is grown. Unripe grass or grass grown in northern climates is likely to contain more THC acid than THC. The acid is not psychoactive, but upon drying much of it converts to active THC by a natural process known as decarboxylation. Most of the remaining acid will convert to THC during a period of two years. Unfortunately, much of this THC will oxidize in this much time. If the decarboxylation could take place in an oxygen-free environment, oxidation would not simultaneously occur. The application of heat can further decarboxylate unconverted THC acids in the dried product. During smoking, although much of the THC and its acid are destroyed by the flame, all that reaches the smoker's lungs has been converted to the active form of THC. If the material containing the

THC acids is heated to about 212°F (boiling temperature of water) for 75 minutes in a nitrogen or carbon dioxide atmosphere (one free of oxygen), all of these acids will convert to THC. Traditional cannabis recipes often call for the sautéing of the ganja in oil or butter before using it. The oil protects the product from the oxygen while the heat activates the THC. This activation also occurs in the extraction of hash oil from weed and in any hash manufacturing procedures where heating or boiling is involved.

Let us attempt to summarize what we know of the effect of heat on cannabis. **While too much heat or overcooking can destroy THC activity, normal cooking temperatures for normal cooking times can increase potency by activating the THC.**

The author was once invited to a dinner at the country home of some friends who were growing their own. The *pièce de résistance* was a salad of freshly picked marijuana leaves. The salad chef very thoughtfully gave these greens a thorough dousing with olive oil to aid in the assimilation of the high. We all ate copious amounts of the salad before dinner. It was fragrant and quite palatable, but none of us got even slightly stoned. At first we thought that it was simply poor grass, but later when we smoked some that we had dried in the sun, we realized that it was one of the best homegrown harvests we had ever had. Even the lower leaves were good. Now we understand why this happened. This grass, grown in a northern climate, contained, in its fresh state, most of its THC in the form of its acid precursor. Since it had not been dried to convert the acids to THC, we might as well have been eating lettuce. Of course, the idea of eating a big bowl of marijuana leaves was a turn-on of its own.

CANNABIS AND APPETITE

A point which should not be overlooked in any treatise on cannabis cooking is the appetite-stimulating property of this substance. This phenomenon has been noted both in clinical studies and in private use. The smoking of grass will often give the user a good case of the munchies. But when it is ingested, it may very well turn him into a gastronomical nymphomaniac. Some grasses are more inclined to do this than others. So when you are consuming cannabis, don't let your cupboard be bare.

We should also point out that food can bring you down. If you are excessively stoned and want to come down a ways, a good meal, a decent snack, or just a tablespoon of honey in warm water will usually put your feet nearer to the ground.

As we have mentioned earlier, too much food in a cannabis dish can defeat your high before it even has a chance to happen. Furthermore, some people—especially those with weak digestive systems—may get a bit queasy when trying to digest cannabis products. The stomach often tries to reject that which is difficult to digest. Too much food may worsen this condition. Even if you are one of the majority who has no problem digesting cannabinated cuisine, too much food in the tummy can be damnably distracting when you are trying to experience euphoria.

CANNABIS AND TASTE

Many of the ancient and modern cannabis preparations are, for the most part, attempts at covering up the taste of marijuana, which many persons find disagreeable. Majoon is a typical example of this approach. It is a confection sweetened and amply spiced with cinnamon, cloves, cardamom, nutmeg or other condiments which adequately, if not thoroughly, disguise the hemp flavor. Some of these recipes have been included here because they are delectable and dependable, not to mention classical.

Most of the author's own recipes, however, are devised upon the premise that the flavor of cannabis is delicious if prepared correctly and combined with other ingredients which are harmonious with its essence. Many of these recipes treat cannabis as a condiment without which the flavor of the preparation would doubtless suffer.

Preparing
Cannabis Material

AVAILABLE CANNABIS PRODUCTS

Cannabis products are derived from the female Cannabis sativa or C. indica plant. The psychoactive substance in cannabis is called tetrahydrocannabinol (THC). In India and other Eastern countries cannabis products come in four basic forms: ganjah (the resin covered flower tops), bhang (the leaves from below the tops), charas (the resins gathered from the tops), and hashish or mimea (the resins extracted with fat in boiling water and solidified). Some of these names mean different things in different locales. The terms bhang and hashish, in some places, are given to intoxicating beverages made from cannabis.

In the United States and most Western nations the available cannabis products are marijuana, hashish and hash oil. The term marijuana refers to all usable parts of the plant. The whole flower tops with little or no broken leafy material is usually the most potent and expensive form of this product. This broken leafy material may be either shakes (the potent crumblings from the dry tops) or the less potent leaves from the lower parts of the plant. A typical sample of decent quality marijuana sold on the American black market would consist of approximately equal portions of tops and shakes with a substantial amount of seeds included.

The term hashish here includes both the fat-extracted hashish or mimea and the gathered charas resins. The term charas is rarely used in America. Sometimes this product is wrongly called kif or pollen hash. Kif is actually a blend of ganjah and black tobacco prepared in Morocco. Pollen, of course, comes from the male, rather than the female, plant. Hashish may be 5 to 8 times as potent as the marijuana from which it was derived.

Hash oil is a solvent extraction of the active oils and resins from either hashish or marijuana. There are different grades of hash oil determined by the degree of refinement and the percentage of active THC. Brown oil is the crudest extraction, but it may be 2 to 4 times as concentrated as the hashish from which it came. Higher refinements include red oil, amber oil, honey oil, and white oil, in that order.

A modern technique known as isomerization may further increase the potency of hash oil without reducing its volume. This treatment of the product was originally achieved by Dr. Roger Adams and reported in the *Journal of American Chemistry Society* (volume 63, page 2211: This process converts one of the inactive components of the oil to active THC and at the same time transforms the lower rotating THC molecule to a higher rotating and more potent isomer. These conversions may increase the potency by as much as six times and also improve the quality of the high. Isomerization removes much of the heavy sleep-inducing characteristics from cannabis and allows a more buoyant and uplifting high. Practical methods for carrying out this isomerization process are given in *Cannabis Alchemy—*

Making High Potency Hash Oil by David Hoye, available from the Twentieth Century Alchemist P.O. Box 3684, Manhattan Beach, California 90266.

PREPARATION OF BASIC MATERIAL FOR CANNABIS RECIPES

The following concoctions are useful in the preparation of fast-acting and potent cannabis recipes. It is not absolutely necessary, however, that all of these materials be on hand. Perhaps the most useful and most easily-prepared among these is canna-butter. This substance is also known as Sacred Ghee in India, where it has been in use for thousands of years.

PREPARATION OF GHEE

Many recipes from India call for the use of ghee. Ghee is clarified butter. In India it is made from water buffalo butter, but any butter will do. Ghee was invented by our Eastern ancestors as a way of preventing the butter from becoming rancid in the absence of refrigeration. Properly prepared ghee can be kept at room temperature or in a moderately cool place for many months without spoiling. It has a mildly tangy butterscotch flavor, which becomes less pronounced the more it is filtered.

There are two basic methods for preparing ghee: skimming and precipitating. The skimming method is accomplished by heating a pound or more of fresh butter in a saucepan at a medium-low temperature, but hot enough that it boils and produces a froth at the top. This froth is skimmed from the surface with a spoon, and discarded. Light boiling is continued and further skimming is done until no more froth appears. It may be necessary to tilt the saucepan at an angle to remove the last particles of froth. The remaining butterfat is ghee. It should be poured into a jar while molten, capped, and stored in a cool place. If it is kept in the refrigerator, it will last even longer. This type of ghee will have a strong butterscotch flavor.

To prepare ghee by the second method, a wok is recommended, but any pot will do. If a wok or cast iron pan is used, it must be absolutely clean. If it is not, the ghee will blacken and taste of metal oxides. To clean the wok place a handful of salt and a little salad oil inside the bowl and scour with the aid of a cloth or paper towels. Repeat with fresh salt and oil until no more oxides appear on the towel. Wipe the remaining salt away with cloth or towels. Never use water to clean a wok or cast iron pan.

Melt 1 or 2 pounds of butter in the wok at medium-low temperature. Allow the molten butter to simmer for a while. White particles will float to the top. Stir frequently to insure that nothing sticks to the bottom. Eventually the butter will start to bubble over. Remove the wok from the stove and let it stand for about five minutes. During this time, the white particles will sink to the bottom. When they have settled, pour the ghee into a jar. If a purer form of ghee is desired, it may be filtered while hot through several layers of cheesecloth. The more it is filtered, the less butterscotch flavor it will have.

The color of cooking ghee is slightly darker than

gold. If it gets any darker than this, your wok or pot is too hot. While the ghee is cooking, steam will rise from it. There will be less volume to the ghee than the original amount of butter.

You may use either salted or unsalted butter to make ghee. The salt and other non-fat impurities are the particles which are removed. Sweet butter is more costly than the salted product, and, unless it is kept in the freezer, it tends to become rancid more quickly. Ghee made from rancid butter has a horrible taste and is bad for you. If you use unsalted butter to make ghee, the residue will have a dark color and a strong butterscotch flavor. It is quite tasty when mixed with honey. If salted butter is used, the residue will be too salty to eat.

PREPARATION OF CANNABUTTER (THE SACRED GHEE OF INDIA)

Melt 1 pound of butter or ghee in a saucepan. Add to this several ounces of finely sifted marijuana. Simmer and stir for a few minutes until the butter takes on the greenish color of the grass. Pour the butter through a fine strainer. While pouring, hold the leafy mash at one corner of the pan with a tablespoon. Tilt the pan slightly and press the mash firmly to squeeze out as much butter as possible. A little heat may be applied beneath the mash to help the butter to flow out better. Strain the salvaged butter which collects in the lower corner of the pan. If absolutely no debris is wanted in the butter, it should be strained through a piece of muslin or several layers of cheesecloth. However, if this is done, much of this active butter may be lost by absorption. Do not discard the leafy material. It still contains considerable resins. It can be simmered in milk or vodka and sweetened with honey or sugar to make a tasty and effective beverage. Hot milk or vodka may also be used to salvage cannabutter from the straining cloth.

More sifted leaf can be heated in the strained cannabinated butter if extra potency is desired. Much of the first batch of cannabutter will get soaked up by the second batch of grass. Strain and salvage as before and attempt to recover as much cannabutter as possible from the mash. Again, the milk or vodka beverage can be prepared from it.

Pour the cannabutter into a jar, cap it, and store in refrigerator or freezer. If ghee has been used, it may be kept in a cool cupboard when refrigeration is not available. Cannabutter can be kept for very long periods in the refrigerator if water is poured over it. The water and cannabutter should be chilled before this is done to prevent any butter from dislodging and floating to the top. The water will remain on top of the butter and act as an oxygen shield.

A simpler and more potent cannabutter can be made by blending the melted butter or ghee with hashish or hash oil instead of grass. It is not necessary to heat the mixture as long as when the grass is used. Just heat and stir until all of the hash or oil dissolves in the butter. Because it dissolves so easily, as much hash or oil can be added as the chef desires. Furthermore, there is no residual pulp to be concerned about. Just dissolve and stir the ingredients together and it is ready for use or storage.

CANNABUTTER FROM SEEDS

The outer portion of marijuana seed hulls is fairly rich in THC. The inside of the seed contains only protein, moisture, and the nonactive fixed oil. The seeds are quite nutritious and have been used by man for food in some parts of the world (also by canaries all over the world). The finest thing that can be done with good seeds, of course, is to plant them. This, for various reasons, is not always practicable.

Cannabutter can be prepared by simmering 1 cup of seeds in ½ pound of butter or ghee at a low temperature for about 5 minutes. Because of their nonporous texture it is easier to strain the butter from the seeds than from the leaves. Also there are hardly any essential oils or terpenes on the seeds. The resultant cannabutter is virtually tasteless and can be used either by persons who do not favor the taste of cannabis, or to surreptitiously turn on a parent, teacher, boss, governor, president, etc.

ETHICAL COMMENTARY

A principle of ethics should be pondered before attempting to stone anyone without their consent. To deny a person his right to use marijuana or any other substance is to deny him his personal sovereignty and freedom of choice in matters which concern only his own body, mind and soul. To stone an unconsenting subject is merely the reverse side of the same coin. A person must always have the right to decide what will or will not be taken into his own body. Without the realization and preservation of this most essential and private freedom, all other freedoms and rights have little or no significance.

POOR RICHARD'S CANNABUTTER

If one has a collection of fine twigs culled from his marijuana siftings, these can be used to prepare cannabutter in much the same way that the seeds were used. If larger stems are all that are available, a preparation can be made using oil instead of butter as the solvent.

Pour a cup of salad oil or coconut oil into a blender. Turn it on to "Chop" speed. Cut up or break stems to lengths not exceeding two inches. Add these to the spinning blender a pinch at a time. When no more stems can be added to the oil without clogging the rotors, pour everything—oil and stem pulp—into a saucepan and heat for ten minutes. Strain the oil and return it to the blender. Repeat the process using new stems and a little more oil to compensate for that which was lost in the first extraction. It is possible to repeat this process several times until the oil is totally saturated. The final preparation is strained and kept under refrigeration in a bottle or jar. It can be used in most recipes which call for cannabutter.

If you have rich friends who use a lot of grass, ask them to save their seeds and stems for you.

ANOTHER COMBINATION

In Nepal and Tibet, hashish is often made by boiling ganja (marijuana tops) in water with fat. The mixture is stirred constantly. Afterwards the liquids are allowed to cool. The fat, which contains the active resins, floats to the top and solidifies. It is then skimmed from the watery solution, which contains the unwanted debris and chlorophylaceous material. Aside from being a practical way of separating the fat-soluble resins from the water-soluble wastes in almost the same step as the extraction, this arrangement has several other advantages. The boiling temperature of water is lower than that of oils and fats. Prolonged, high-temperature boiling in unwatered fat might decompose much of the active material. The water keeps the temperature down to a relatively safe level. Furthermore, the water increases the total volume of the boiling solution, thereby allowing more marijuana to go into the cauldron. If the cauldron were filled with fat, the result would be a lot of fat containing weak concentrations of THC. With the water/fat combination the active oil-soluble materials are concentrated into the small percentage of fats present in the brew. Because the water-soluble portions of some crops of marijuana are harsh-tasting and acrid to the throat, it may be desirable to apply this practice in the preparation of cannabutter. It is not always necessary, however, being largely a matter of your personal taste and the type of grass used. Thoroughly chew and swallow a pinch of your grass. If it causes an unpleasant burning sensation in the mouth and throat, you will most likely want to remove the water-soluble components by this method.

Fill the boiling pot ⅓ the way with crushed and crumbled marijuana tops. Fill the pot ¾ the way with 1 part butter, fat, or oil and 4 or more parts water. Boil this for 30 minutes. Stir frequently. With a poaching spoon, remove as much debris as possible from the bottom. Allow the liquids to cool to room temperature, then place the pot in the refrigerator. The butter on top will harden and can be removed in one piece. If oil has been used instead of butter, it will be necessary to use the freezer to solidify it.

If a still stronger product is desired, the cannabinated oil or butter can be recombined with fresh water and more grass and the entire process repeated. Another possibility is to use cannabutter which has been prepared by the non-water method as the fatty base for this butter/water extraction.

The method of separating can also be applied to salvage cannabutter which has turned out to be harsh and acrid. In this case boil 1 part cannabutter for 10 minutes in 2 parts water. Allow liquids to cool to room temperature. Refrigerate or freeze for an hour and remove the block of purified cannabutter from the top. Much of the harsh materials will have separated into the watery portion and can be discarded.

A similar procedure may be employed to remove any harsh-tasting substances from cannabis tar. A volume of tar is boiled for 10 minutes in 5 volumes of water, cooled to room temperature and refrigerated for an hour or so. Do not freeze in this case or you may have to chop through ice to retrieve much of your tar. While still cold, remove solidified chunks of tar from the water. Be certain that all of the tar is recovered. Save the tar; discard the water.

PREPARATION OF CANNABIS TAR

Place ½ pound of marijuana (seeds and stems may be included) in a large double boiler or heat bath, cover with alcohol (about two quarts), and boil for 45 minutes. If available, pure grain ethyl alcohol may be used. If not, vodka is a fair substitute since it contains about 50% ethyl alcohol in water. These are expensive solvents in countries where liquor taxes are high. Because all of the alcohol will be removed by evaporation before the tar is used, one may use isopropyl rubbing alcohol instead. It contains 70% isopropyl alcohol and 30% water. In the USA, it is much cheaper than vodka or pure grain spirits. Be sure to use no kind of rubbing alcohol other than isopropyl compound. This is the kind that is usually sold. Some rubbing alcohols are ethyl alcohol with a bitter nauseant added to discourage drinking. Do not use this latter type, as it will leave a horrid-tasting residue.

Keep a constant watch on the boiling pot. Be cautious not to let the alcohol boil over. Remember that alcohol boils at a lower temperature than water. Also remember that alcohol is combustible. It is safer to use a hot plate or electric range than a gas burner for this process.

After 45 minutes, strain the boiled materials and save the green solution (the extractions). Add more alcohol to the mash while it is still damp and repeat boiling for another 45 minutes. After straining the second extractions, combine them with the first ones. A third extraction may be carried out. But since its active content will be rather low, it is best to save this extraction to be used as the first extraction solvent the next time you make tar.

Fill a clean double boiler half way with the strained extractions. Heat these without a lid and under well-ventilated conditions until the liquids have boiled down to about one-quarter way. Add more extractions to bring liquids back to the halfway mark. When the last of the extractions are in the pot, continue boiling until the scent of alcohol is no longer detectable. The problem at this point is to evaporate off any remaining moisture without scorching the tar. If 100% pure alcohol is used, this problem does not exist, since double boiling may be continued until only the tar remains. If vodka or rubbing alcohol is used, there will be a considerable water content which must be removed. There are two practical methods of achieving this.

The boiled-down extracts can be poured into a pyrex baking dish and left in an oven overnight with the heat at the lowest possible setting. In the morning, if all moisture is gone, the tar can be scraped up while still warm and put up in a jar.

The alternate method requires more effort but less time, if you are in a hurry. Fill the lower compartment of the double boiler with salad oil rather than water. Be sure that the pot is completely dry. Otherwise the oil may spatter when heated. Heat the double boiler as before, but at a slightly higher temperature. Oil boils at a higher temperature than water. You may continue boiling off the water until it is gone, without scorching the tar. When evaporation is completed, pour the molten tar into a jar. Any which clings to the pot can be loosened by adding some hot vodka. This vodka solution can be sweetened with honey and served as a cordial or used as a stoning cooking brandy.

CANNABIS COOKING BRANDY

Since cannabis resins are very soluble in alcohol and also easily assimilated in that medium, an excellent way of introducing them into many dishes is through the addition of a cooking brandy or rum which has been well saturated with hemp products. This cooking brandy is not at all similar to Creme de Gras, for which a recipe is given later. Creme de Gras is a delicately flavored liqueur made from marijuana. Cannabis cooking brandy is not intended for pleasurable drinking. It can be used in any recipe that would call for a rum or brandy, such as mince pie, rum babas, rum- or brandy-soaked pound cakes, and even egg nogs, which contain sufficient egg-milk-nutmeg mix to ameliorate that somewhat coarse and overwhelming character of the cooking booze. Cannabis brandy is a handy item to have in the cupboard around the holidays. And holidays are great to have any time of the year.

The preparation of this brandy is quite simple. Place whatever cannabis materials you have on hand and wish to use in a mason jar. These may be anything from your best flowering tops to leftover stems, seeds, roaches (with paper removed), siftings too fine to smoke, and general debris. Cover these with rum, brandy, or even vodka if you prefer. Allow them to soak at least a week. After soaking, place the mason jar in a hot bath as shown in the illustration. Loosen the top to allow the escape of expanding fumes. Heat for 30 to 45 minutes. Strain the liquids while hot and pour them over new seeds, stems, etc. Repeat the soaking, heating and straining process as before. The repetition may be continued three or four times until the liquor has been thoroughly saturated with resins and is too dense to extract any more. Strain after the final extraction and put it up in a bottle for use. If you have any scraps of hashish, these can be added to the final product after it has been strained and while it is still hot. The hashish should be pulverized or shaved before adding. Similarly, if you have any remnants of hash oil clinging to the walls and bottom of its former container, these can be loosened by adding some hot brandy, etc., and swirling it about. This may then be added to the strained liquor. Do not add hashish or hash oil to the unstrained liquids. Much of it would only get lost among the stems and debris. After the first straining, the soggy hemp materials should be returned to a mason jar and covered with fresh brandy. There are still some resins in these materials that are worth salvaging. The remains from subsequent strainings can be soaked in the salvaging liquids after these liquids have been strained. These liquids may eventually be used to extract fresh materials. With a few mason jars in the cupboard, a continuous extracting process can be maintained and nothing will be wasted.

Shake the bottle of cannabis brandy well before using. Much of the active material will have settled to the bottom. If the solution is supersaturated, some resins may precipitate in gummy lumps which do not redissolve upon shaking. If this is the case, heat the cooking brandy in a hot bath, shake gently until dissolved, and add the brandy to the recipe while still hot. Do not have the heat on while the bottle is in the bath, or it may crack. Bring the pot of water to a boil and turn off the heat. Warm the base of the bottle under hot running water for two minutes, and stand the bottle in the bath for five minutes. Repeat the entire process, if necessary. Keep the bottle top loosened so that the expanding air and vapors can escape.

Recipes

The following recipes contain no meat, fowl or fish. This is because of a personal prejudice of the author who feels that the slaughter of animals for food is unnecessary, uneconomical and unhealthy. He does not wish to encourage the carnivorous act by giving recipes which contain meat. But neither does he wish to proselytize his readers with his private opinions. Therefore, to the meat eaters who use this book he will state only that any animal fat such as lard will serve the same function as vegetable oil, butter or ghee. To those who are even more strict in their vegetarian practices than himself and refrain from dairy products, he suggests that Crisco or any vegetable oil can be used in place of butter fats.

The amounts to be used of the various ingredients are fairly flexible and should be adjusted to personal tastes. The quantities of marijuana, hashish or hash oil recommended in these recipes may be even more subject to variation. THC potencies of grass which is either grown locally or smuggled in, may range between 1 and 5 percent. The potency of hashish may vary just as extremely (6 to 10%). That of hash oil, because of different methods of manufacture and refinement, as well as adulteration by unscrupulous dealers, may fluctuate even more widely.

Approximate amounts of the cannabis materials to be used in these recipes are given on the assumption that they are of good, average potency. The reader must determine the precise amount of these substances to use on the basis of potency of available materials, individual tolerance, and the degree of intoxication desired.

BHANG

The term bhang usually refers to the larger leaves and capsules without stalks of the female hemp plant. These are also known as subjee or sidhee. Bhang is also a name for an intoxicating (non-alcoholic) beverage prepared in India from these materials in combination with milk (sometimes water) and added flavorings. In some parts of India this beverage is called hashish. The recipe varies from one province to the next. The two following recipes are from *On the Preparation of the Indian Hemp, or Gunjah* by W.B. O'Shaughnessy, reprinted from *Transactions of the Medical and Physical Society of Bengal*, 1838–40.

Sidhee, subjee, *and* bang *[synonymous] are used with water as a drink, which is thus prepared. About three tola weight, 540 troy grains, are well washed with cold water, then rubbed to powder, mixed with black pepper, cucumber and melon seeds, sugar, half a pint of milk, and an equal quantity of water. This is considered sufficient to intoxicate an habituated person. Half the quantity is enough for a novice. This composition is chiefly used by the Mahomedans of the better classes.*

Another recipe is as follows:
The same quantity of sidhee *is washed and ground, mixed with black pepper, and a quart of cold water*

added. This is drank at one sitting. This is the favorite beverage of the Hindus who practice this vice, especially the Birjobassies, and many of the rajpootana soldiery.

From either of these beverages intoxication will ensue in half an hour. Almost invariably the inebriation is of the most cheerful kind, causing the person to sing and dance, to eat food with great relish, and to see aphrodisiac enjoyments. In persons of quarrelsome disposition it occasions, as might be expected, an exasperation of their natural tendency. The intoxication lasts about three hours, when sleep supervenes. No nausea or sickness of stomach succeeds, nor are the bowels at all affected; next day there is slight giddiness and vascularity of the eyes, but no other symptom worth recording.

A modern approach to making a highly assimilable and potent bhang-type beverage has been devised by the author.

HOT BUTTERED BHANG

In a saucepan, melt half a cube (⅛ pound) of butter or ghee. Crumble a good handful of marijuana tops or leaves (⅓–½ ounce). Stir the grass into the molten butter. Continue stirring over medium heat for one minute. While it is hot and sizzling, add 8 ounces of vodka. Be cautious that the hot butter does not make the mixture spatter. It is best to pour in the vodka swiftly. Continue to boil for 30 seconds or more, stirring all the while. A pinch or two of powdered cardamom seed may be added during the boiling. You may wish to experiment with other spices, such as cinnamon, clove or nutmeg. Or you may prefer no added flavorings.

Another choice which you have is the alcoholic content of the beverage. It may have the spirit potency of a hot buttered rum, or it may be boiled a little longer to give it the strength of a hot mulled wine. If you are a total teetotaler, you may boil it until all of the alcohol is gone. One may ask, in this case, why water was not used instead of vodka. It should be remembered that alcohol efficiently extracts the cannabis resins. When the alcohol is completely evaporated off, the resins remain dissolved in the residual water. If one plans to remove all or most of the alcohol, some water should be added to compensate for volumetric loss.

After boiling as much as desired, strain the liquids. Press the mash in the strainer with the back of a spoon to remove all of the juices. Discard mash or boil it again in fresh vodka to salvage more materials. Sweeten to taste with honey if wanted. Pour the liquids into 4-ounce wine glasses. Top with whipped cream if desired and garnish any way that you like. Serves two.

This recipe is not only an efficient method of extracting the active principles from marijuana, and an excellent medium for assimilation (alcohol, butter and honey), but it also has a delicious and satisfying flavor. It is reminiscent of hot chocolate, but is much more pleasant to drink. It is one of the most swiftly absorbed cannabis concoctions. The effects of the grass may be felt in less than fifteen minutes. Cheers!

INSTANT HASH BHANG

For those who are not inclined to lavish in lengthy rituals when preparing food, drink, or cerebral sacrament, the previous recipe may appear somehwat task-ridden. Actually it is not much more involved than making coffee from the beans. Even that would seem complicated and messy to one who has not yet learned. There are those, of course, who have only the patience for instant coffee. Instant hash bhang is the drink for them! Although a coffee connoisseur would not touch the instant product with a ten-foot teaspoon, instant hash bhang is as fine a brain-boggling beverage as hot buttered bhang, or even the original and classical bhang of the Hindu provinces. It calls for hashish, but requires no alcohol or lengthy extraction, since the active substances are already concentrated in the hashish and are readily dissolved in the hot buttered water. It is an ideal beverage for seduction, so again we make the recipe for two persons.

Add a half-inch slice of butter to two cups of water boiling in a small pot. Shave or crumble ½ to 1 gram of hashish into this, and let it boil slowly for one minute or more. Fill two 8-ounce parfait glasses (or any vessels that won't crack from heat) one-third the way with milk. Strain equal amounts of the hashish concoction through a fine-mesh strainer into the glasses and save the residues in the strainer. The cold milk should keep the hot brew from cracking a glass. Add honey, fructose, or artificial sweetener. Flavor with cinnamon, nutmeg, vanilla extract, almond extract, or any item of this sort.

The small amounts of hash residues in the strainer still contain usable materials and can be added to the decoction the next time it is prepared. Some hashish leaves no residue at all. This is preferred. If hashish is not available, hash oil, cannabis tar, or possibly even cannabis cooking brandy could be substituted.

MAJOON

Majoon, in some provinces of India, is a potent jam which may be spread on crackers, used as a pastry filling or eaten by the fingerful. One way to prepare it is: Toast ¼ ounce of cleaned marijuana tops on a dry skillet over low heat until golden brown. Be careful not to scorch it. Pulverize the toasted grass with 1 cup chopped dates, ½ cup raisins or currants, ½ cup ground walnuts, 1 teaspoon each of ground nutmeg, anise seed, and ginger, and ½ cup honey. Cook the mixture with ½ cup of water (add more if needed) until the ingredients have softened and can be blended together. While hot, add 2 tablespoons of melted butter or ghee and stir for 5 minutes. Seal in a jar and keep under refrigeration.

HAMENTASHEN

This is another jam which is made with hashish that may be used in the same ways as majoon.

Mix 2 cups of prune or apple butter, ½ cup of ground almonds, 1 tablespoon of lemon juice, ½ to 1 teaspoon of powdered cinnamon, and ¼ ounce of powdered hashish. Thoroughly blend the ingredients. Seal in a jar and refrigerate.

Majoon and Hamentashen are similar to the so-called green paste consumed at the famed Club des Haschischins of Paris during the 1800's by such notables as Baudelaire, Gautier and Rimbaud.

MAJOON CANDY

Majoon sometimes takes the form of candies. One such recipe was given to Dr. O'Shaughnessy by his friend Ameer.

Four ounces of sidhee, and an equal quantity of ghee are placed in an earthen or well-tinned vessel, a pint of water added, and the whole warmed over a charcoal fire. The mixture is constantly stirred until the water all boils away, which is known by the crackling noise of the melted butter on the sides of the vessel. The mixture is then removed from the fire, squeezed through cloth while hot—by which an oleaginous solution of the active principles and colouring matter of the Hemp is obtained—and the leaves, fibres, etc. remaining on the cloth are thrown away.

The green oily solution soon concretes into a buttery mass, and is then well washed by the hand with soft water, so long as the water becomes coloured. The colouring matter and an extractive substance are thus removed, and a very pale green mass, of the consistence of simple ointment, remains. The washings are thrown away: Ameer says that these are intoxicating, and pro-

duce constriction of the throat, great pain, and very disagreeable and dangerous symptoms.

The operator then takes 2 lbs. of sugar, and adding a little water, places it in a pipkin over the fire. When the sugar dissolves and froths, two ounces of milk are added; a thick scum rises and is removed; more milk and a little water are added from time to time, and the boiling continued about an hour, the solution being carefully stirred until it becomes an adhesive clear syrup, ready to solidify on a cold surface; four ounces of tyre [new milk dried before the sun] in fine powder, are now stirred in, and lastly the prepared butter of Hemp is introduced, brisk stirring being continued for a few minutes. A few drops of attur of roses are then quickly sprinkled in, and the mixture poured from the pipkin on a flat cold dish or slab. The mass concretes immediately into a thin cake, which is divided into small lozenge-shaped pieces. A seer thus prepared sells for four rupees: one drachm by weight will intoxicate a beginner; three drachms, one experienced in its use: the taste is sweet, and the odour very agreeable.

MARRAKESH WHITE COOKIES

Blend together 1 cup of warm cannabutter and ½ cup of sugar or honey. Beat in one egg. Stir in 2 teaspoons vanilla extract. For variation almond, orange or lemon extract may be used; or any combination of these. Sift together 3 cups of flour and 1 teaspoon of baking powder. Combine ingredients to make dough.

Chill the dough in the refrigerator for an hour until firm. Roll the dough to about ¼-inch thickness. Cut into 1- or 2-inch circles. A small drinking glass may be used if a cookie cutter is not available. Place the cookies on a baking tray or cookie sheet, press an almond into the center of each cookie, and bake in a preheated oven at 375° for 6 to 8 minutes.

THC PBC's

This stands for tetrahydrocannabinated peanut butter cookies. The oil in the peanut butter as well as the butter dissolves the resins in the grass during cooking, so it is not necessary to make any preparatory materials.

In a mixing bowl combine 2 cups of flour, 1½ cups of peanut butter, 2 or 3 eggs, ¾ of a cup of honey, 1 cup of butter (at room temperature), 1 teaspoon of baking soda, ½ teaspoon of salt, and 2 ounces of finely sifted marijuana. If extra potency is desired, cannabutter may be used in place of butter. Blend these ingredients thoroughly. Place cookie-size droppings of the batter on a baking tin, and press lightly on each cookie with the back of a fork several times to flatten them. Bake for 10 or 12 minutes in a preheated oven at 375°. Don't overcook.

Hashish or hash oil may be used in place of (or as well as) marijuana. Other nut butters can replace the peanut butter.

CANDY BUDS

Tribes in the Rif mountains of Morocco often roast whole stalks of freshly harvested marijuana outdoors over a fire, turning them frequently and taking care not to burn the leaves and flowertops. These are then sprinkled with salt, dipped in honey, and eaten off the stalk. The following is a more sophisticated recipe based upon the practice of these tribes.

The tops of high quality, freshly dried marijuana often have a fragrant, balsamy flavor. Persons who are aware of this will occasionally chew up a bud for an offbeat taste treat and a pleasant high. The effectiveness and flavor of these buds can be enhanced by candying them in the following manner:
Select a number of small- to medium-size buds (2- to 4-inch lengths). Choose a grass that is tasty, easy to chew and which leaves no acrid aftertaste. Slightly immature buds with few or unripened seeds make matters easier. If the grass is fairly fresh and not dried out and crumbly, the seeds can be removed by lightly rolling the bud between the thumb and forefinger. Most of the seeds will fall right out of the bud. Seeds that are more difficult to remove can be loosened and popped out with the thumbnail. When the seeds are out, take a piece of string and tie a loop around the stem of each bud. Loops should be at least two inches apart to insure that the buds not stick together.
In a small saucepan over low heat, melt a few tablespoons of ghee (or cannabutter if you want extra strength). Tilt the saucepan so that the butter collects in one corner. Briefly dip each bud into the molten

butter. Keep it submerged no more than a second or two. You want to soak the bud with butter, but not extract any of the resins into the butter. Swish the bud around while submerged so that the butter gets to the in-between places. Suspend the string for 15 minutes to allow excess butter to drip from the buds.

Dip each bud in honey. Move the bud up and down in the honey to coat it thoroughly. Again suspend the string of buds and allow honey to drip. Keep this in a place where it will not attract flies or ants. After a week, the honey will have hardened somewhat. It may then be dipped a second time. After another week of drying, the honey will again be somewhat hardened. The buds may then be eaten or allowed to hang longer.

This is an excellent way of preserving the potency of the buds. The coating of honey protects the THC from oxidation. If the grass was fairly fresh or if it came from a northern environment, it may have much of its THC present in the form of THC acid. If this is so, the bud may increase in potency while it is stored because much of the THC acid will convert to active THC. If faster conversion is desired, the buds may be placed in an oven for one hour at no higher than 225°F immediately before the second honey dipping. If buds are to be kept for a long time, they should be allowed to harden for several weeks after the last honey dip and then be wrapped in foil or plastic wrap.

Candy buds are a tasty and stony confection which preserves the original fragrance of the grass. Different grasses will have different flavors. Thai sticks, sinsemilla, Panama red, Kona gold, and light green Michoacan are good choices. Experiment, have fun, and chew your candy buds well for best results.

ACAPULCO GREEN

Although it is nowhere as ancient as majoon, bhang or hamentashen, this recipe from Mexico has at least become classical in its own time. It is a stoning type of guacamole or avocado dip. The standard recipe is as follows: Mix 3 tablespoons of wine vinegar, 2 teaspoons of chili powder and ½ cup of pulverized marijuana. Let the vinegar-moistened materials stand for 1 hour. Add 3 ripe avocados and ½ cup of chopped onions. Mix all ingredients well until avocados are mashed and all materials are evenly blended. Serve as a dip with corn chips. This is a tasty and effective recipe, but the author of this book believes that it can be somewhat more effective if vinegar is not used in preparing the marijuana and chili powder. The acid vinegar lessens the solubility of the cannabis resins to some extent. An alternate method of preparing this dip is to heat the grass in a saucepan for several minutes with ½ cup of olive oil. The grass/oil can then be blended with the avocado, onion and chili mixture. A little lemon juice adds a tang to the dip, but will not inhibit THC assimilation as would the vinegar.

HASH OIL HONEY

A number of underground vendors of cannabis products in the United States have been offering their clientele hash oil in various ready-to-eat forms. The most popular among these are cannabinated candy bars and hash oil honey. In order to prepare either of these delicacies, the hash oil must first be rendered miscible by dilution in oil or butter fat. The author prefers to use ghee for this because of the tangy butter-scotch flavor which it imparts to the honey.

In a small saucepan at a low temperature heat 1 tablespoon of ghee, butter or vegetable oil for each gram of hash oil to be combined. Stir in hash oil until it is thoroughly blended with the fat. If it is difficult to dissolve, the temperature may be raised a little. When the products are evenly combined, ½ cup of honey is added to the oil for each gram of hash oil. The honey and the oil are stirred over heat until thoroughly blended. The product can be poured into a jar while still hot and allowed to cool before capping. One tea-spoon of this honey is usually sufficient for a high. It can be eaten straight from the jar, spread on crackers, or dissolved in a cup of hot water to make a stoning hot beverage: Hash Oil Tea.

HASH OIL CANDY BARS

The ghee and hash oil blend can also be used to make an organic type candy bar as follows: Combine ½ cup each of chopped dates, raisins, figs, and ground al-monds with 1 teaspoon each of ground aniseed, nut-meg and ginger. These can be heated slightly and 4 tablespoons of the hot hashish/butter blend can be combined with the above ingredients. The mixture is then cooled, kneaded or rolled, and cut into individual candy bars. These may be wrapped individually in waxed paper, foil or plastic. Or the ingredients can be combined with 1 cup of water, heated, and blended, before stirring in hash oil/butter. The mixture is then heated at a low temperature and stirred constantly to prevent scorching. When this mixture has thickened to a workable consistency, it is spread on a well-greased baking tin and placed in an oven at 225°F for 30 minutes or until hard enough to cut into individual squares. Some of these candy bars being sold in the underground market come in printed wrappers stating the exact amount of hash oil per bar. Some manufacturers add a gram of powdered ginseng to each bar. The ginseng counterbalances some of the mind-boggling effects of the candy and helps the consumer to maintain better under its influence.

EASY CANDY BALLS

This recipe requires no special preparations of the cannabis material. It can be made from plain marijuana, hashish or hash oil. Furthermore, it requires no cooking. The oils present in the nut butter serve as a medium for the cannabis resins.

Combine ½ pound nut butter (I prefer cashew or almond to peanut) with 1 ounce or more of finely-sifted marijuana, or ½ to 1 ounce of pulverized or finely-shaved hashish, or 5 to 15 grams of hash oil. Add a few tablespoons of honey in accordance with the sweetness of your tooth, and small amounts of anything else that pleases: dried currants, shredded coconut, ground orange or lemon peel, powdered cloves or nutmeg, etc. Knead these ingredients until thoroughly blended. Roll into individual balls about the size of a large marble. These should be wrapped individually in waxed paper, foil, or transparent wrap, and kept under refrigeration to prevent the nut butter from becoming rancid. One or two candy balls should be a ball.

CANNABIS MILKSHAKE
(AND ICE CREAM TOO)

Combine ½ ounce or more of finely-pulverized marijuana leaves and flowers (no seeds or stems) with a pint of half-and-half (half cream and half milk). Add a level teaspoon of lecithin granules. Mix these in a blender for 1 or 2 minutes. Pour the contents of the blender into a saucepan and heat gently for 10 minutes in a double boiler. Do not overcook, or curds will separate from the milk. Stir in several tablespoons of honey while the mixture is hot. Pour the mixture into the blender jar, add ½ teaspoon of vanilla extract, cover the top, and refrigerate for several hours until chilled. When you wish to drink it, put it on the electric blender again for 30 seconds and serve in a glass with a straw.

If you want to make it into ice cream, add a raw egg and whip thoroughly in the blender until frothy. Pour into any suitable vessel, such as an empty cottage cheese or ricotta container, or into individual custard cups. Put a lid on the containers, or cover the cups with waxed paper or plastic wrap, and place these in the freezer. Do not wait too long before freezing, or the whipped texture will settle to its original liquidy state.

If you prefer, this ice cream or shake can be made with hashish or hash oil. To do so, first dissolve hashish or hash oil in a small amount of butter or ghee.

Then add it to the half-and-half/lecithin mixture as before. A euphoric sundae can be made by covering this ice cream with cannabis chocolate icing.

CANNABIS CHOCOLATE ICING

If you crush a bud of freshly dried marijuana between your fingers, you may notice a chocolate-like aroma mingled among its fragrances. There is no real similarity between cocoa beans and cannabis. The likeness is only in our perceptions. But it is strong enough that a high grade of aromatic grass grown in Mexico is referred to—at least in that country—as chocolate (pronounced cho-ko-lah-tay). It is possible to take advantage of this curious similarity and apply it in certain recipes such as the following:

Melt 4 ounces of cannabis tar in a double boiler. Add one teaspoon or more of vanilla extract. While stirring, add 4 ounces of honey. Thoroughly blend all of the ingredients. You now have an icing that can be used in bakery recipes of your own selection or invention, such as cannabis layer cake, frosted cupcakes, stoned-out ice cream topping; or you can just spread it on crackers. It's so damned finger-licking good that you may never even get past the finger-licking stage. This icing tastes amazingly like chocolate icing, but twenty minutes or so after eating it, you'll never remember a chocolate cake that made you feel this way. A tangy variation can be made by adding a teaspoonful of orange extract during the stirring.

HOT COCOA-TYPE BEVERAGE

Heat 1 pint of whole milk or half-and-half in a double boiler. When hot, stir in and thoroughly dissolve 1 to 2 teaspoons of cannabis tar, 2 to 4 teaspoons of honey, and 1 teaspoon of vanilla. Some persons may wish to add a pinch of salt. If whole milk has been used instead of half-and-half, and if you are not watching your waistline, you may also add 1 or 2 teaspoons of butter to increase the fat content and aid the assimilation. Serve in cups with a dollop of whipped cream on top. Makes 2 servings.

CURRIED HASH

We have already been advised against combining cannabis with heavy meals. Curry powder is generally used to flavor solid dinners, which are a poor vehicle for ingested highs. Nevertheless, it may be valuable to have on the condiment rack a curry powder which can be used both to spice and spike a light but nourishing dish. This can be prepared by combining 1 part curry powder with 3 or 4 parts powdered hashish. Blond charas is ideal because it powders easily and is similar in color to the curry. Half fill a jar with these two components and shake the jar vigorously for one minute or more to combine the materials homogeneously. A teaspoon of the mixture can be sprinkled upon or stirred into any small dish which is suited to this seasoning. Hot buttered rice or vegetables are most ideal because of the fat content. Another cannabinated curry preparation is described in *The Connoisseur's Handbook of Marijuana* by W.D. Drake, Jr. His recipe, although called Curry Powder, is actually a combination of freshly ground curry spices in cannabinated butter.

ONION SOUP RUDERALIS

This rugged Russian-style soup is named after *Cannabis ruderalis*, the vine-like variety of marijuana found only in parts of Russia.

Sauté four to six thinly sliced onions in a generous portion of oil or butter. When onions are partially cooked, but have not yet begun to brown, stir in ½ to 1 ounce of finely sifted marijuana. Continue to sauté until the onions begin to brown. Remove pan from heat. Sprinkle four tablespoons of flour over the onions and stir in. Cover the pan and let it sit on low heat for five minutes or so. Stir every few minutes. Have ready one quart of heated water. Add the onions to the water. Thoroughly rinse the pan with this water and return these juices to the soup pot. Remember that the fats at the bottom of the pan contain much of the magic ingredient, THC. Add any seasoning that you want. Simmer for thirty minutes. Add a little wine, brandy or (if you feel up to it) cannabis cooking brandy. Serve with a garnish of sour cream, parmesan cheese, paprika, and dill weed. Stir well before serving. See that each guest receives similar proportions of top and bottom fluids. The oil containing the THC tends to rise to the surface.

This soup utilizes the extracting properties of the oil in the same manner that cannabutter does. In this recipe, however, the flavor of the grass becomes integrated with that of the onions. The sour cream adds more fats to aid in assimilation, and the alcohol further assists. If the grass still has any gritty texture left after so much cooking, the sour cream sort of greases the granules and smooths things out.

There are many variations of this recipe, such as using mushrooms, asparagus or whatever instead of, or as well as, onions; or adding cream instead of sour cream. And the choice of spices, of course, is always yours.

CREME DE GRAS

This is a fine cordial or liqueur of the highest caliber. It differs from the earlier mentioned cannabis cooking brandy, which is merely an accumulation of resins in strong liquor. No actual cooking is involved in the preparation of this cordial. The fragrant, balsamy aroma and flavor of fresh cannabis are entirely preserved. After some experience the connoisseur cordial maker will realize that different types of grass will impart distinctly different essences to the liqueur, and that he can make from these a wide variety of cordials, each with its own characteristic qualities, much as the vintner does with different grapes. He may, also like the vintner, eventually experiment with blending different stocks of cordial.

This may be the most important recipe in this book. Not only will the liquor industry make billions from it after this brief period of marijuana prohibition has ended, but it may even play a major role in the survival and evolution of the human race. Now, all us radical, dope-smoking hippies know that if we could turn on our parents, teachers, bosses, governors, presidents, etc., everything would mellow out, wars would stop, and the Aquarian Age would descend upon us in a white cloud. The difficulty, of course, is in getting these rigid pillars of reality to have anything to do with the vile weed. Well, all of us hippies who are really hip known the way to a straight person's heart is through his bottle. So don't forget to invite old dad over for a drink around the holidays (see *Ethical Commentary* on page 25).

Place 2 ounces of marijuana (all parts may be used) in a one-quart mason jar. Completely cover the grass with heated vodka or a similar mixture of pure grain spirits and distilled or spring water (50/50). Cap the jar and keep it in a moderately warm place for at least five days. Check it occasionally to see that all of the grass remains submerged. Strain, and save the liquids in a bottle. Resoak the mash in fresh vodka for another five days or so. Strain the liquids and combine them with the first strainings. Cover the mash this time with distilled or spring water and let soak for another five days but no longer than that. On the final day, heat the jar in a pan of boiling water for 45 minutes. See that the jar cap is loosened before heating. Strain the liquids while hot and add them to the other liquids. Filter the combined liquids through a conical paper coffee filter. Because of the large amount of fine debris suspended in these liquids, it will be necessary several times to replace clogged filter papers with fresh ones.

If any murkiness remains in the filtered liquors, bottle them and let them stand undisturbed for about a week while the sediment settles and the liquid above it becomes clear. Siphon the clear liquors off of the sediment. Put these liquors in a clean mason jar with a slightly loosened cap and heat in a pan of boiling water for about 15 minutes or until the liquors warm to about 180°F. Stir in honey until the desired sweetness is attained. Pour the liquids through a funnel into a clean bottle; the taller and more slender the bottle, the better. Allow it to stand for several months; the longer, the better. More sediment will precipitate. Carefully, so as not to disturb the sediment, siphon the clear liquids into a clean bottle. Label it Creme de Gras. It is about 50 or 60 proof. One or two cordial glasses of it won't get you drunk, but if you are willing to wait about fifteen minutes, it is guaranteed to get you high.

RETSINA SATIVA

The Greeks add resin to their wine for flavoring and call it *retsina*. Why then can't we do the same with the active resins of Cannabis sativa? Well, we can. But there is one minor obstacle to be coped with. The 11 to 13% alcohol in wine is too weak to get the resins to dissolve in sufficient quantities to have any effect other than altering the taste. This problem can be overcome by first dissolving the resin in a small amount of heated pure grain alcohol, vodka or brandy. A highly concentrated hash oil is the best material to use, because you get more THC into each wineglass without burdening the wine with heavy solids and overwhelming tastes. Two or more grams of hash oil can be dissolved in one ounce or more of heated alcohol. This solution is added immediately, while still hot, to a ⅕-quart bottle of white wine at room temperature. Shake well to spread the resin evenly through the wine. Hashish may be used if hash oil is not available. Break up four or more grams of hashish and dissolve in four or more ounces of hot alcohol. Hashish does not dissolve as easily as hash oil. Some extra stirring and repeated heating may be required. When the material is dissolved, add it to the wine as before. Each ounce of pure grain alcohol added to the bottle of wine will increase the total percentage by volume of alcohol in the wine by a factor of 4 percent. One ounce of pure grain spirits in ⅕ quart of wine which contains 11% alcohol will raise the wine's alcohol content to 15%. Each ounce of 100-proof vodka or brandy will increase the wine's alcohol content another 2%. Four ounces of vodka or brandy added to a ⅕-quart bottle of 12% table wine will bring its alcohol content up to about 20%, which is the same as that of a heavy wine such as port or sherry. One or two wineglasses of retsina sativa should do the trick.

CANNABEER

During the early 1940's, researchers Warmke and Davidson were seeking ways of improving cannabis hemp fiber for the war effort. The Japanese had cut off supply lanes for Manila hemp. They attempted to graft marijuana plants to hops rootstocks (hops is marijuana's only known relative). Unfortunately for the war effort, none of these grafts took. When they reversed the procedures, however, and grafted the hops plants to the marijuana stocks, the graftlings survived and flourished. When mature they were plants with all the outward appearances of the legal hops vine. They even had the aroma and bitterish flavor of the hops. But they contained as much of the psychoactive THC as any marijuana plant. In 1970, this obscure piece of information was given to the public by Mary Jane Superweed (*nom de plume*) in *The Super Grass Grower's Guide*, and by William Drake, Jr. in *The Connoisseur's Guide to the Cultivation of Cannabis*. Since that time, the federal government has become concerned over the numbers of grass farmers who are grafting to produce undetectable cannabinated hops plants. The Department of Agriculture has issued instructions (not laws) to all hops growers and suppliers to sell no hops plants to anyone who is not in the commercial hops-farming business or beer industry. Hops is used for flavoring beer. It contains a substance called lupuline which is chemically related to THC, but is not nearly as potent. It tends to act as a mild sedative. It is the hops which also gives to beer its relaxing and sometimes sleep-inducing qualities.

The question has been posed: What would happen if one were to use for beer-making, hops which had been grafted to marijuana stocks? Would one be able to get a marijuana high from a bottle of beer? One may possibly get stoned from such a beer if the stocks are from very high-potency grass such as that which comes from Thailand, Nepal or Afghanistan and it is grown in the best soil and climate. One of the difficulties would be to extract enough of the cannabis resins from the hops fruits. The oil-soluble resin does not dissolve in watery beer. The alcohol content of even the strongest beer is insufficient to dissolve the resins. To insure the THC potency of such a brew one should first do a concentrated extraction of the cannabinated hops fruits into hot vodka or ethanol. This can be added to the beer after it is brewed (or purchased). It is not good to introduce the alcohol to the beer during brewing because it may stop the process of fermentation. If cannabinated hops are not available, a marijuana/alcohol extraction can be combined directly with a bottle of commercial beer. Experiment with different amounts. Try to achieve a balance of not too much vodka or ethanol to get you drunk, but enough cannabis potency to get you high. Recently, some authors have refuted the findings of Warmke and Davidson regarding the presence of THC in grafted hops. Their point is that the methods used by these researchers to determine the presence of THC were not valid. Until this question has been resolved, it may be a waste of time for the reader to attempt the graft.

CANNABIS AND COFFEE

In some Eastern and North African countries, hashish is added to coffee. It has been noted that this combination increases the effects of the hashish, but diminishes its duration. In his paper, "On the Hashish or Cannabis Indica," in *The Boston Medical and Surgical Journal,* April 16, 1857, John Bell, M.D. mentions this phenomena and suggests that it may be due to a more rapid absorption of the hashish. There is a probability, however, that the caffeine and related substances in coffee have something to do with these effects. Drugs frequently potentiate each other. Caffeine may enhance the stimulating properties of cannabis. Since the first effects of cannabis include stimulation, the caffeine may augment these effects during the initial stage. This stimulation usually turns to drowsiness after several hours. Coffee is, of course, an effective antidote for lethargy. Many seasoned hedonists, especially those with leisure, find that a joint and a cup of coffee is a most perfectly balanced combination for starting the morning right; stimulating enough to get one into the day, but sufficiently mellowing to keep one from being wired.

There are several ways in which coffee can be spiked with cannabis. A most delightful and exotic morning cup is made as follows:

TURKISH EYE-OPENER

Prepare a pot of good coffee. In a Turkish coffee pot place one teaspoonful of finely-powdered straight Arabian mocha for each cup. This coffee and the Turkish pot can be purchased from any vendor specializing in quality teas and coffees. Add a pinch of powdered cardamom seed and one-half gram of pulverized hashish for each cup. Pour the amount of coffee desired over the powdered mocha and cardamom. Heat the Turkish pot over a low flame until it threatens to bubble over. Remove it from the heat immediately. Serve in demitasse or espresso cups with a small spoon. Dissolve a teaspoon of honey in each cup. This is the way that Turkish coffee is served whether with or without hashish. The coffee is sipped from the top and the powdered mocha, honey and whatever is eaten like candy from the bottom with the spoon.

Other possible cannabis/coffee combinations include:

LEPRECHAUN'S DELIGHT
(IRISH-STYLE COFFEE)

To a cup of coffee add a shot of Creme de Gras and top with whipped cream. If you're a truly rugged Son of Ireland with a stomach like that of Patrick's pigs, you might wish to substitute a thick shot of cannabis cooking brandy for the Creme de Gras.

JACK TAR COFFEE

Dissolve a gram of cannabis tar in a cup of very hot coffee. It won't really dissolve unless you add some alcohol, but it will be sort of suspended in the coffee. Add some heavy cream right away. The fat content of the cream will render the tar more soluble and will aid in its assimilation. You may add a little honey to make this beverage more palatable. But remember, too much sugar will slow down the digestion of the fat. It should also be pointed out that regular use of coffee with cream and sugar is not very good for one's liver.

BUTTERBALL COFFEE

Stir into a cup of coffee one or more teaspoons of strongly concentrated cannabutter. Butter in coffee may sound weird, but many people do it and dig it. So don't knock it till you've gagged on it.

HASH OIL AND COFFEE

Several drops of hash oil can be dissolved in a hot cup of coffee with cream added.

TEAS TO EASE THE HASH-PARCHED THROAT

Although we have offered many lung-saving recipes throughout this book, most of us will continue to smoke our cannabis products. Even this author, for all his good advice, has yet to end the practice entirely. So long as we must smoke, let us do so in relative comfort.

In Eastern countries where hashish is smoked in such abundance that hacking, rasping and wheezing almost seem to be the national language, various teas are served to lessen the soreness and give to the throat at least the illusion of coolness and comfort.

One of the most popular of these Moroccan teas is a blend of 2 parts black tea, 3 parts spearmint leaves, and 1 part hibiscus flowers. The mint has a cooling and soothing effect upon the throat. The black tea and hibiscus together act as a mild and pleasant astringent. The black tea also contains 2% caffeine, which helps to counter the effects of overindulgence. This tea should be steeped, but not boiled. Most sharply aromatic herbs, such as mint and wintergreen, owe their qualities to volatile oils which will vaporize and be lost if boiled. Boil the tea water first. When it is bubbling, remove it from the heat and allow 30 to 60 seconds for it to cool a few degrees before pouring it over the leaves in a teapot. Let it steep for two or three minutes before serving. Hibiscus is interestingly tart, but you may want to sweeten the tea with honey. Honey also acts as a demulcent, lining the throat and giving soothing protection against the smoke. White sugar is not a good demulcent and may even worsen some throat irritations.

When I prepare Moroccan tea, I often substitute rose hips for hibiscus. They have much the same taste, but the rose hips contain vitamin C and some rutins and bioflavinoids. Vitamin C is depleted in the body from smoking. The rose hips help to replace it. Furthermore, the vitamin with the rutins and bioflavinoids helps to rebuild the ruptured capillaries of a sore throat and strengthens them against future damage. Rose hips are also a mild astringent. It is difficult to extract the benefits of rose hips by merely steeping them. They should be crumbled and put into the boiling water. This is afterwards poured over the black tea and mint leaf mixture.

OTHER TEAS WHICH YOU CAN INVENT

The ideal hash-smoker's tea blend consists of a soothing aromatic, a demulcent, a healing agent, and a mild astringent. A mild expectorant may also be included, as well as any palatable herb which serves as an anti-spasmodic.

Among the demulcent herbs are: anise, star anise, licorice, sassafras, slippery elm bark, coltsfoot, comfrey root, flaxseed; marshmallow flowers, leaves and roots; honeysuckle flowers.

Among the soothing aromatic herbs are: peppermint, spearmint, thyme, sage, wintergreen, cardamom seeds, cloves, cinnamon, allspice, eucalyptus leaves, angelica seed, hyssop, ginger root, coriander seeds, and catnip.

If cinnamon is to be used, break up pieces of the stick. If powdered cinnamon is used for teas, it releases a gelatin-like substance which gives the tea a slimy texture. The small amount of this material from the broken stick cinnamon has the the advantage of serving as a demulcent. Licorice and marshmallow root produce a similar mucilaginous material and should be used sparingly and not be boiled too long. Marshmallow leaves yield less of this mucilage than the root, and the flowers even less.

Among the mild astringent herbs are: thyme, sage, rosemary, comfrey root and leaves, ginseng, elecampane.

Another healing agent with a tart tang like hibiscus and rose hips is pure vitamin C. It is available in the powdered form from many health stores and some pharmacies. It is a good lemon substitute. ⅓ teaspoon equals 1,000 mg. Most people prefer no more than a pinch (300–500 mg) per cup. If it is too tart, it can be sweetened with honey.

Among the expectorant herbs are: horehound, mullein flowers, goldenrod leaves, lungwort, forget-me-not leaves.

Sage milk is prepared in many Mediterranean countries and drunk for its pleasant taste and its favorable influence upon the respiratory organs. It is simply sage leaves boiled in milk and strained. Some people sweeten it with honey.

In Java and other places hibiscus flowers are boiled in coconut milk and allowed to cool before serving as a very palatable beverage for easing coughs and throat inflammations.

Ginseng is an excellent tonic for the nerves, blood circulation, and glands. It also helps the body to heal itself more swiftly. If one is planning to party heavily and smoke or consume immoderate amounts of cannabis, substantial doses of ginseng root or ginseng tea, taken several hours beforehand, will enable a person to so indulge and yet maintain his equilibrium.

Besides being a good demulcent, honeysuckle flowers also have antispasmodic properties.

For the Reader

FOR THOSE WHO
HAVE READ THIS BOOK

The aim of this book has been to teach the reader all that he needs to know in order to make his own decisions when preparing foods and beverages with cannabis products. With this knowlege he may become inventive in devising recipes which suit his personal taste. All that the author can now recommend is that the reader keep the foregoing information in mind, exercise his imagination, experiment freely, and enjoy.

POSTSCRIPTS

After submitting the manuscript of this book to the publisher, the author continued (and still continues) to experiment with his subject. At some future date, his findings may add several chapters to a later edition of this work. In the meantime, the author wishes to share these findings with his readers rather than withhold them until such chapters are written. For now these additional points will be offered as brief notations.

A variation of Hot Buttered Bhang can be made without the use of alcohol. Its potency is equal to the recipe containing alcohol, but because of the absence of that substance it takes just a little longer to assimilate into the system.

Other flavorings which can be added to Hot Buttered Bhang: Coconut extract, Chocolate extract, instant chocolate (adds sweetening too), mint extract (just a few drops), or creme de menthe (mint goes well with Chocolate).

After drinking enough alcohol to cause a hangover, one may ingest cannibis, retire, and wake up feeling fine.

Persons who often wake with stiff muscles may injest cannabis before retiring and awake in the morning without stiffness.

Powdered hashish or charas may be blended with Tahini (sesame butter) which is then made into halvah using any standard recipe for this confection.

RONIN

Books for Independent Minds

GROWING MARIJUANA HYDROPONICALLY .... Hans $14.95 ___
Sea of green, perpetual harvest for cottage techniques.
MARIJUANA LAW .... Boires $17.95 ___
Eveything you need to know to protect your rights and avoid getting busted.
PASS THE TEST .... Potter/Orfali $16.95 ___
An employee guide to drug testing, tells how to beat the test.
CANNABIS UNDERGROUND LIBRARY .... 7 rare classics $16.95 ___
Marijuana and hashish, history, cultivation, preparation, treasured secrets.
MARIJUANA BOTANY .... Clarke $24.95 ___
Sexing, cultivation, THC production and peak potency, continued production.
MARIJUANA CHEMISTRY .... Starks $24.95 ___
Species, seeds, grafting, and cloning, growing techniques and essential oils.
CANNABIS ALCHEMY .... Gold $14.95 ___
Classic and modern techniques to enhance potency and prepare hash.
CULTIVATOR'S HANDBOOK OF MARIJUANA .... Drake $24.95 ___
Land and light concerns, harvesting and curing, psychoactive tobacco.
MARIJUANA HYDROPONICS .... Storm $18.95 ___
Equipment lists, diagrams, step-by-step set-up for high-yield system.
PSYCHEDELICS ENCYCLOPEDIA .... Stafford $38.95 ___
LSD, peyote, marijuana and hashish, mushrooms, MDA, DMT, yage, iboga, etc.
GROWING EXTRAORDINARY MARIJUANA .... Gottlieb $12.95 ___
Simple, easy methods to grow pot.
DR. ATOMIC MARIJUANA MULTIPLIER .... Todd $12.95 ___
How to turn pot into high potent hash.
PSYCHEDELIC UNDERGROUND LIBRARY .... 9 rare classics $24.95 ___
LSD, peyote and other cacti, mushrooms, cocaine, DMT.
MARIJUANA FOOD .... Drake $14.95 ___
Guide for the sensuous connoisseur. Recipes for meals and massage oils.
LEGAL HIGHS .... Gottlieb $12.95 ___
All kinds of readily available highs to enjoy without risk of being busted.
AMAZING DOPE TALES .... Gaskin $14.95 ___
Incredible stories from Stephen Gaskin—the most famous hippy.
START YOUR OWN RELIGION .... Tim Leary $14.00 ___
How to write your own New Testiment and select your sacrament for worship.
HEALING MAGIC OF CANNABIS .... Potter/Joy $14.95 ___
It's the high that heals! How faith, hope & cannabis helps healing.

Books prices: SUBTOTAL $_____

CALIF customers add sales tax 8.75% $_____

BASIC SHIPPING: (All orders) $5.00

Make sure to add in the per book shipping fee - essential!

Plus SHIPPING: add USA+$1/bk, Canada+$2/bk, Europe+$7/bk, Pacific+$10/bk $_____

Books + Tax + Basic + Shipping: TOTAL $_____

MC _ Visa _ Disc _ Exp date _ _ - _ _ card #: _

Phone # (Req for CC orders)_ _ _ _ _ _ _ _ _ _ _ _ _ _ _ Signature_ _ _ _ _ _ _ _ _ _ _ _ _ _

Name_ _

Address _ _ _ _ _ _ _ _ _ _ _ _ _ _ _ _ City _ _ _ _ _ _ _ _ _ _ _ _ _ State _ _ _ ZIP _ _ _ _

Make checks payable to **Ronin Publishing, Inc.**

POB 22900, Oakland, CA 94609 • Ph: 800/858-2665 • Fax: 510/420-3672

orders@roninpub.com • www.roninpub.com • Catalog online

Call for free catalog • Wholesale queries welcome • Prices subject to change w/o notice